BOOKWORMS

Silver

STORIES FOR READING CIRCLES
Stage 2 (700 headwords)
Stage 3 (1000 headwords)

The seven short stories in this book come from different volumes in the Oxford Bookworms Library. There are five stories at Stage 2 and two stories at Stage 3. All have been specially chosen for Reading Circles.

There is something to please everybody, from Sherlock Holmes detective stories, to the horror stories of Edgar Allan Poe, or the gentle family stories of H. E. Bates. There are English authors and American authors; classic authors such as Thomas Hardy, and modern authors such as Jan Mark. There are stories about New Yorkers, a father worrying about his daughter, a young woman wanting to get married, and a teenage boy who plays in a rock band and who has a problem with his father.

OXFORD BOOKWORMS LIBRARY
Series Editor: Jennifer Bassett
Founder Editor: Tricia Hedge

BOOKWORMS CLUB

Silver

STORIES FOR READING CIRCLES

Editor:
Mark Furr

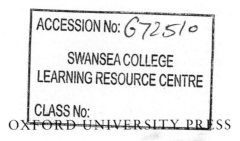
OXFORD UNIVERSITY PRESS

OXFORD
UNIVERSITY PRESS

Great Clarendon Street, Oxford OX2 6DP

Oxford University Press is a department of the University of Oxford.
It furthers the University's objective of excellence in research, scholarship,
and education by publishing worldwide in

Oxford New York

Auckland Cape Town Dar es Salaam Hong Kong Karachi
Kuala Lumpur Madrid Melbourne Mexico City Nairobi
New Delhi Shanghai Taipei Toronto

With offices in

Argentina Austria Brazil Chile Czech Republic France Greece
Guatemala Hungary Italy Japan Poland Portugal Singapore
South Korea Switzerland Thailand Turkey Ukraine Vietnam

OXFORD and OXFORD ENGLISH are registered trade marks of
Oxford University Press in the UK and in certain other countries

'Too Old to Rock and Roll' from *A Can of Worms and Other Stories* by Jan Mark
Original edition © Jan Mark 1990 First published by The Bodley Head 1990

'Go, Lovely Rose' by H. E. Bates Original story © Evensford Productions Ltd

This simplified edition © Oxford University Press 2007
Database right Oxford University Press (maker)

6 8 10 9 7 5

ISBN 978 0 19 472001 4

Printed in China

ACKNOWLEDGEMENTS

Oxford University Press is grateful to Laurence Pollinger Ltd on behalf of
Evensford Productions Ltd for permission to simplify the story 'Go, Lovely Rose'

CONTENTS

SOURCE OF STORIES

The seven stories in this book were originally published in different volumes in the OXFORD BOOKWORMS LIBRARY. They appeared in the following titles:

The Christmas Presents
O. Henry, from *New Yorkers*
Retold by Diane Mowat

Netty Sargent and the House
Thomas Hardy, from *Tales from Longpuddle*
Retold by Jennifer Bassett

Too Old to Rock and Roll
Jan Mark, from *Too Old to Rock and Roll and Other Stories*
Retold by Diane Mowat

A Walk in Amnesia
O. Henry, from *New Yorkers*
Retold by Diane Mowat

The Five Orange Pips
Sir Arthur Conan Doyle, from *Sherlock Holmes Short Stories*
Retold by Clare West

The Tell-Tale Heart
Edgar Allan Poe, from *Tales of Mystery and Imagination*
Retold by Margaret Naudi

Go, Lovely Rose
H. E. Bates, from *Go, Lovely Rose and Other Stories*
Retold by Rosemary Border

~

Welcome
to Reading Circles

Reading Circles are small groups of students who meet in the classroom to talk about stories. Each student has a special role, and usually there are six roles in the Circle:

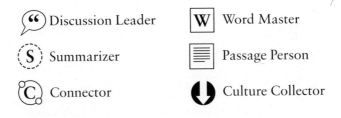

(") Discussion Leader | **W** Word Master

(S) Summarizer | **≣** Passage Person

(C) Connector | **↓** Culture Collector

Each role has a role sheet with notes and questions which will help you prepare for your Reading Circle discussions in the classroom. You can read more about the roles and the role sheets on pages 77 to 83 at the back of this book.

The stories in this book have been specially chosen for Reading Circles. They have many different themes, and students everywhere enjoy reading them and talking about them in their Circle. Everybody's ideas are important; there are no 'right' or 'wrong' answers when you are talking about stories.

Enjoy the reading, enjoy the talking – and discover the magic of Reading Circles . . .

Mark Furr
Hawaii, May 2006

The
Christmas
Presents

~

What are presents for? We give presents on special
days like birthdays and name days, and festivals
like Christmas. But why do we do it? Do we give
presents because we want to show how rich we
are? Or how generous we are?

Della and Jim are young and happy, and very
poor. The next day is Christmas, and Della wants
very much to give her Jim a present, a wonderful
present, something really special. But she has only
one dollar and eighty-seven cents . . .

O. HENRY

The Christmas Presents

Retold by Diane Mowat

One dollar and eighty-seven cents. That was all. Every day, when she went to the shops, she spent very little money. She bought the cheapest meat, the cheapest vegetables. And when she was tired, she still walked round and round the shops to find the cheapest food. She saved every cent possible.

Della counted the money again. There was no mistake. One dollar and eighty-seven cents. That was all. And the next day was Christmas.

She couldn't do anything about it. She could only sit down and cry. So she sat there, in the poor little room, and she cried.

Della lived in this poor little room, in New York, with her husband, James Dillingham Young. They also had a bedroom, and a kitchen and a bathroom – all poor little rooms. James Dillingham Young was lucky, because he had a job, but it was not a good job. These rooms took most of his money. Della tried to find work, but times were bad, and there was no work for her. But when Mr James Dillingham Young came home to his rooms, Mrs James Dillingham Young called him 'Jim' and put her arms round him. And that was good.

Della stopped crying and she washed her face. She stood

by the window, and looked out at a grey cat on a grey wall in the grey road. Tomorrow was Christmas Day, and she had only one dollar and eighty-seven cents to buy Jim a Christmas present. Her Jim. She wanted very much to buy him something really fine, something to show how much she loved him.

Suddenly, Della turned round and ran over to look in the glass on the wall. Her eyes were bright.

Now, the James Dillingham Youngs had two very special things. One was Jim's gold watch. It once belonged to his father, and, before that, to his grandfather. The other special thing was Della's hair.

Quickly, Della let down her beautiful, long hair. It fell down her back, and it was almost like a coat around her. Then she put her hair up again, quickly. For a second or two she stood still, and cried a little.

Then she put on her old brown coat, and her old brown hat, turned, and left the room. She went downstairs and out into the road, and her eyes were bright.

She walked along by the shops, and stopped when she came to a door with 'Madame Eloise – Hair' on it.

Inside there was a fat woman. She did not look like an 'Eloise'.

'Will you buy my hair?' Della asked.

'I buy hair,' Madame replied. 'Take your hat off, then, and show me your hair.'

The beautiful brown hair fell down.

'Twenty dollars,' Madame said, and she touched the hair with her hand.

'Quick! Cut it off! Give me the money!' Della said. The next two hours went quickly. Della was happy because she was looking round the shops for Jim's present.

At last she found it. It was a gold chain for The Watch. Jim loved his watch, but it had no chain. When Della saw this gold chain, she knew immediately that it was right for Jim. She must have it.

The shop took twenty-one dollars from her for it, and she hurried home with the eighty-seven cents.

When she arrived there, she looked at her very short hair in the glass. 'What can I do with it?' she thought. For the next half an hour she was very busy.

Then she looked again in the glass. Her hair was now in very small curls all over her head. 'Oh, dear. I look like a schoolgirl!' she said to herself. 'What's Jim going to say when he sees me?'

At seven o'clock the dinner was nearly ready and Della was waiting. 'Oh, I hope he thinks that I'm still beautiful!' she thought.

The door opened and Jim came in and closed it. He looked very thin and he needed a new coat. His eyes were on Della. She could not understand the look on his face, and she was afraid. He was not angry or surprised. He just watched her, with that strange look on his face.

Della ran to him.

'Jim,' she cried. 'Don't look at me like that. I sold my hair because I wanted to give you a present. It will soon be long again. I had to do it, Jim. Say "Happy Christmas", please. I have a wonderful present for you!'

'You've cut off your hair?' asked Jim.

'Yes. I cut it off and sold it,' Della said. 'But don't you love me any more, Jim? I'm still me.'

Jim looked round the room.

'You say your hair has gone?' he said, almost stupidly.

'Yes. I told you. Because I love you! Shall I get the dinner now, Jim?'

Suddenly Jim put his arms round his Della. Then he took something from his pocket and put it on the table.

'I love you, Della,' he said. 'It doesn't matter if your hair is short or long. But if you open that, you'll see why I was unhappy at first.'

Excited, Della pulled off the paper. Then she gave a little scream of happiness. But a second later there were cries of unhappiness.

Because there were The Combs – the combs for her beautiful hair. When she first saw these combs in the shop window, she wanted them. They were beautiful combs, expensive combs, and now they were her combs. But she no longer had her hair!

Della picked them up and held them. Her eyes were full of love.

'But my hair will soon be long again, Jim.'

And then Della remembered. She jumped up and cried, 'Oh! Oh!'

She ran to get Jim's beautiful present, and she held it out to him.

'Isn't it lovely, Jim? I looked everywhere for it. Now you'll want to look at your watch a hundred times a day.

Give it to me! Give me your watch, Jim! Let's see it with its new chain.'

But Jim did not do this. He sat down, put his hands behind his head, and he smiled.

'Della,' he said. 'Let's keep our presents for a time. They're so nice. You see, I sold the watch to get the money to buy your combs. And now, let's have dinner.'

And this was the story of two young people who were very much in love.

WORD FOCUS

Perhaps Della was thinking about her present for Jim while she waited for him to come home. Complete the passage with these words. (Use one word in each gap.)

*belonged, chain, combs, face, home, important, long, loves, present,
ready, sees, sell, show, watch, when, without*

'Well, dinner's nearly _____ now, and Jim will be _____ soon. I'm so excited about my wonderful Christmas _____ for him. I hope he likes it. I know he loves his gold _____. His father gave it to him _____ he was eighteen, and before that the watch _____ to his grandfather. This gold _____ will be just right for it. I know he'll look at it every day. I didn't want to _____ my beautiful long hair because Jim _____ my hair. But what could I do? Jim must have a Christmas present because Christmas _____ presents is terrible. I loved my _____ hair, too. But I had no pretty _____ to wear in it. And Jim is more _____ than my hair – I wanted to buy him something really beautiful, something to _____ how much I love him. I can't wait to see his _____ when he _____ my present. Oh . . . here he comes now . . .'

STORY FOCUS

Match these halves of sentences to make a paragraph of eleven sentences.

1 Jim and Della were poor, . . .
2 One was Jim's gold watch . . .
3 On the day before Christmas, when Della counted her money, . . .
4 After Della looked at her hair in the mirror, . . .
5 When she sold her hair, . . .
6 Then, Della looked around the shops . . .
7 When Jim came home and saw Della, . . .
8 After he put his arms around Della, . . .
9 When Della opened the package, . . .
10 Finally, Della gave Jim the chain, . . .
11 Jim told Della that he sold his watch, . . .

12 . . . he had a strange look on his face.
13 . . . she saw the beautiful combs for her long hair.
14 . . . because he needed money to buy her present.
15 . . . Jim gave her a present.
16 . . . but he did not get out his watch.
17 . . . and the other was Della's beautiful hair.
18 . . . but they had two special things.
19 . . . and she bought a fine chain for Jim's gold watch.
20 . . . she got twenty dollars.
21 . . . she was sad because she had very little money for Jim's
    Christmas present.
22 . . . she decided to sell it.

Netty Sargent
and the House

If you want to get married, you need somewhere
to live. And in England in the 1890s, if you were
poor, you usually had to live with your family –
until they died.

Netty Sargent is a pretty young woman with
black hair and dancing eyes. She lives with her old
uncle in a nice house, and she wants to get married
to a young man called Jasper. Jasper likes Netty,
but he also likes her uncle's house very much. And
Netty's uncle doesn't like Jasper . . .

Netty Sargent and the House

Retold by Jennifer Bassett

Netty Sargent lived with her uncle in that lonely house just outside the grounds of the squire's big house. She was a tall young woman, with black hair and dancing eyes. And she had a little laughing smile that sent all the young men wild. All the young men of that time were after her, but in the end she decided that Jasper Cliff was her favourite. He was good-looking, but he only ever thought about himself, not other people. But Netty wanted Jasper, and none of the others. Jasper liked Netty too, but he was more interested in her uncle's house.

The house was built by Netty's great-great-grandfather, and had a garden and a little field next to it. But it was a leasehold house, because the ground belonged to the squire.

'And what happens,' Jasper asked Netty one day, 'when your uncle dies?'

'The house, garden and field will go back to the squire,' said Netty. 'But if Uncle pays a few pounds, he can renew the leasehold and put another name on it. Then the squire can't get the house back until that person dies.'

'And what is your uncle going to do?' asked Jasper.

'Oh, he's going to renew the leasehold, and put my name on it. He told me that months ago.'

Netty's uncle knew that it was important to renew the

leasehold, because the squire was very anxious to get the house back. The squire didn't like all those little leaseholds on his ground, and he wanted to pull the house down and make it all nice and tidy.

Netty's uncle knew this very well – but he still didn't renew the leasehold. He didn't like Jasper Cliff, so perhaps he didn't like to think of Jasper marrying Netty and living in the house when he was dead.

Every week Jasper asked Netty about the leasehold, and Netty asked her uncle, and her uncle said, 'I'll go and see the squire's agent next week.' But still nothing happened.

At last old Mr Sargent fell ill, and Jasper got tired of waiting. 'Why doesn't your uncle do it?' he asked Netty. 'I tell you, if you lose the house and ground, I won't marry you. And there's an end of it.'

Poor Netty hurried indoors to talk to her uncle.

'Please do something, Uncle!' she said. 'If I don't get the house, I won't get a husband!'

'And you must have Jasper, must you, my dear?'

'Yes, Uncle, I must!'

Old Sargent didn't want to make Netty unhappy, so he asked for a meeting with the squire's agent. The squire was very cross when he heard this. He was hoping that old Sargent would die and the leasehold would come to an end. But he had to agree to renew the leasehold if Sargent paid the money. So the squire's agent got the new papers ready for old Sargent to sign.

By now Netty's uncle was really ill, and couldn't leave the house. The agent agreed to visit him. 'I'll come at five o'clock on Monday,' he told Netty, 'and Mr Sargent can pay the money and sign the papers then.'

At three o'clock on that Monday Netty brought her uncle a cup of tea. When she came in the room, her uncle gave a little cry and fell forward in his chair. Netty ran to him, but he could not speak or move. And in a few minutes, she saw that his face and hands were cold and white. He was dead, stone-cold dead.

Netty was very unhappy. 'Why didn't he live two more hours?' she thought. 'Now I've lost everything – house, garden, field, and a home for myself and my lover. What *am* I going to do now?'

Then, suddenly, she knew what she had to do. It was a dark December afternoon, which was very helpful for her. First, she locked the front door. Then she moved her uncle's table in front of the fire. Her uncle's body was still in his chair, which was a big old chair on wheels. So she pushed the chair, with her uncle in it, to the table, putting the chair with its back half-turned to the window.

On the table she put the large family Bible open in front of him, and put his finger on the page. Then she opened his eyes a little, and put his glasses on his nose. When it got dark, she lit a candle and put it on the table beside the Bible. Then she unlocked the door, and sat down to wait.

When she heard the agent's knock at five o'clock, she hurried to the door.

'I'm sorry, sir,' she whispered. 'Uncle's so ill tonight. I'm afraid he can't see you.'

The agent was not very pleased. 'So I've come out all this way for nothing, have I?'

'Oh no, sir, I hope not,' said Netty. 'We can do the business about the leasehold, can't we?'

'Of course not. He must pay the money, and sign the leasehold papers in front of me. I have to be a witness.'

Netty looked worried. 'Uncle is so afraid of business things like this. His hands were shaking when I told him that you were coming today.'

'Poor old man – I'm sorry for him,' said the agent. 'But he must sign the papers, and I must be a witness.'

'Yes, I understand that, sir,' said Netty. She thought for a minute. 'You have to see *him*. But can you still be a witness, sir, if *he* doesn't see *you*?'

'How do you mean, girl?' said the agent.

'Come with me a minute,' she said.

She took him into the garden and round to the window. Inside, the agent could see, at the other end of the room, the back and side of the old man's head, and his arm. He could see the glasses on his nose, and the book and the candle on the table.

'He's reading his Bible, sir,' said Netty, in her softest, sweetest voice.

'Yes, I see that,' said the agent. 'But nobody ever sees him in church, do they?'

'No, but he loves his Bible,' said Netty. 'I think he's sleeping a little at the moment, but that's not surprising in an old man, who's so unwell. Now, sir, can you stand here at the window and watch him sign the papers? Then he won't see you, and he won't be worried and unhappy about it all. Can you do that for him, sir?'

'Very well,' said the agent. He took out a cigar, lit it, and began to smoke. 'Have you got the money ready?'

'Yes,' said Netty. 'I'll bring it out.' She hurried inside, and brought out the money. The agent counted it, then gave Netty the leasehold papers.

'Uncle's hand is very shaky now,' she said. 'And he's so sleepy. I don't think he signs his name very well.'

'He doesn't have to have beautiful writing. He just has to sign,' said the agent.

'Can I hold his hand, to help him?'

'Yes, hold his hand, girl – that'll be all right.'

Netty went into the house, and the agent went on smoking his cigar outside the window. He saw Netty put the pen and the papers in front of her uncle, and touch his arm, and speak to him. She showed him where to write his name on the papers, and put the pen in his hand. Then she stood behind him, and held his hand. But the agent could still see a bit of his head, and he saw the old man's hand write his name on the papers.

Then Netty came out and gave the papers to the agent, and the agent signed his name as witness. He gave her the paper signed by the squire, and left.

And the next morning Netty told the neighbours that her uncle was dead in his bed.

So that's how Netty Sargent lost her house and field, and got them back again – with a husband. But Jasper was a mistake as a husband. After a few years he started hitting Netty – not very hard, but it made her angry. Then she told a neighbour about the leasehold business, and the story got around. By then the old squire was dead, and the squire's son got to hear the story. But Netty was a pretty young woman, and the squire's son never did anything about it.

WORD FOCUS

Match each word with an appropriate meaning. Then use the words to complete the sentences below. (Use one word in each gap.)

to begin something again

agent

to write your name on a letter, important papers, etc.

Bible

an important man who owned a lot of land in and around a village

leasehold

renew

somebody who does business for another person

sign

a person who watches when an important paper is signed, and who also signs the paper

squire

witness

when somebody can use a house or land for a certain time, often many years, before the owner can take it back

the holy book of the Christian Church

1 Netty's uncle did not own the house. The house and garden were _____ because the ground belonged to another man.

2 Jasper wanted Netty's uncle to _____ the leasehold, so he could live in the house when he married Netty.

3 The _____ owned a lot of land around Netty's house, and he wanted to take the house back from her uncle.

4 When the squire's _____ came to Netty's house, her uncle was dead.

5 Netty put her uncle's finger on the page of a large _____.

6 Netty's uncle had to _____ the leasehold papers, so Netty held his hand.

7 The squire's agent was a _____ when Netty's uncle signed the papers.

STORY FOCUS 1

What do you think about the people in this story? Was Netty cleverer than the men? Choose some names from the list and complete these sentences.

Netty / Jasper / Netty's uncle / the squire / the agent / the squire's son

1 I think _____ did a very bad thing when _____.
2 I think _____ was cleverer than _____ because _____.
3 I think _____ was right to _____.
4 I think _____ was wrong to _____.
5 I think _____ made a mistake when _____.

STORY FOCUS 2

Imagine that you are a reporter and you have heard that Netty Sargent did 'something bad' to get her uncle's house. You can ask Netty five questions to find out what she did and why. Which five questions will you ask her?

1

2

3

4

5

Too Old
to
Rock and Roll

~

Do you understand your parents? Do your parents understand you? It's not always easy to be a teenager. Greg is a teenager, he plays in a rock band, and is good at cooking. But one terrible day Greg's mother is killed in a road accident, and Greg's life changes. His father is deeply unhappy, and lives in a sad, silent world. Greg does not know what to do about him. Perhaps his mother's friend Valerie can help – nice, kind, sensible Valerie . . .

Too Old to Rock and Roll

Retold by Diane Mowat

'Why don't you both stop it?' Valerie's voice said on the phone.

'Well, Dad began it,' Greg answered. 'He called me a baby.'

'And you called him an old man. That wasn't nice.'

'I didn't really mean it. He isn't very old, is he?' Greg said. He remembered that Valerie was about forty herself.

'No. And what about that piece from the newspaper about older men losing their hair? You put that up on the kitchen wall! You've got to stop it,' Valerie said.

'We need someone here to stop us,' Greg said quietly.

'I know,' Valerie spoke softly now. 'Well, I'll be there at eight o'clock tonight. I'll see you then, all right?'

Greg put the phone down and went into the kitchen. He looked at the piece from the newspaper about men losing their hair. Near it on the wall there was a piece of paper with Mum's writing on it. Perhaps it was the only thing of Mum's in the house now. Dad took away all her things when she died.

Dad still had a lot of hair. It was only a bit thin on the top of his head. And he did it differently now. It showed that he was getting better after Mum's death. At first he didn't want to do anything. Greg watched him in those first weeks. Dad got up, read the newspaper, cooked meals, went to work – but he was dead inside. When he was at work, Dad was Stephen

Barber the optician. Perhaps there he smiled and talked and was more like a living person. But he wasn't like that at home.

Things were getting better now because of Valerie. She was a friend of Mum's really, and was waiting to see Mum when the unhappy policeman came to the house to tell them about the accident. She lived about fifty kilometres away and had a home to go back to. But the policeman wanted to take Dad and Greg to the hospital and Dad turned to this stranger and said, 'Please stay.' So when they came back, she was there.

And Christmas happened because of Valerie, too. Greg said nothing about Christmas, but one day Valerie said angrily to Dad, 'And what about Greg, Steve?'

'He isn't interested in Christmas,' Dad answered tiredly. 'Christmas was wonderful with Frances. Without her, it's nothing.'

'Well, Frances is dead, but you and Greg are alive. If Christmas with Frances was wonderful, it was because she loved it. Can't you keep alive something she loved? Can't you do it for her?'

Later Greg said to Valerie, 'Are you coming here for Christmas?'

'I usually visit my mother and father,' she replied.

But Greg knew that Valerie must come. 'If Christmas doesn't happen this year,' he thought, 'perhaps it will never happen again.'

'Tell me about Christmas with your Mum, Greg,' Valerie said. And Greg told her how he and his mother always put the decorations on the Christmas tree together.

'I've got all the things for the tree in my room,' he said. 'I hid them there when Dad took everything of Mum's away.'

'Well, we've got to be hard with him,' Valerie said. 'If we want to bring him back to life, we'll have to be a bit unkind to him. Wake him up a little.'

And so, on Christmas Eve, just before Valerie arrived, Greg came downstairs with the box of decorations for the tree.

His father looked old and tired. 'What have you got there?' he said.

'The decorations for the tree,' Greg answered.

'What tree? We aren't having a tree. How could you—'

'*I* want a tree,' Greg said. 'I'm sure that Mum wants Christmas to be happy for me.'

His father looked round slowly. 'It's too late to get a tree now,' he said.

'Valerie's bringing it with her,' Greg replied. 'Shall I light the fire?'

⁂

After Christmas life was easier. Valerie came more often and she stayed for the weekend. They began to call the third bedroom 'Valerie's room'.

Slowly, Dad was beginning to come back to life. He bought some new clothes too, and Greg was pleased about that. But perhaps the piece about older men losing their hair was unkind, Greg thought. He took the piece of newspaper off the kitchen wall, and wrote a note in its place.

I'VE GONE TO BAND PRACTICE. VAL PHONED. SHE'LL BE HERE AT EIGHT.

Then he put the dinner to cook slowly while he was out. The table was ready, with flowers on it, and everything looked

24

just right. Greg usually cooked the meals. He was good at it, and he liked everything to be nice for his Dad and Val.

The band practice was at a friend's house, and Greg began to go there five months after Mum's death. He just wanted to get out of the house sometimes, but he told Dad he was interested in music.

'Music?' Dad said, 'or Rock and Roll?'

'Rock and Roll was in the 1950s,' Greg told him. 'It's rock music these days.'

After the practice that evening, Greg wanted to get home quickly. He wanted to hear happy voices and listen to the nice things that Valerie said about his cooking. So he said goodbye to his friends and hurried home.

The light was on in the living room when he arrived, and for a minute he watched from outside. Dad was standing alone in the room, with his back to the window, but Valerie's car was outside the house. Then Valerie came into the living room, and his father walked over to her with his arms open.

Greg went round to the back door very slowly. He wanted to give them more time together. He felt very pleased that his plan was going well. He liked Valerie a lot, and often told Dad that he liked her. There was no hurry, but if one day Dad and Valerie . . . He would never forget Mum, of course. Sometimes he thought that he could see her in the house or the garden. But he knew that Valerie understood this.

When Greg went in, they were sitting down again. There were a lot of flowers in the room – red, pink, orange and yellow.

'Valerie brought them,' Dad said, smiling.

Greg remembered Valerie's beautiful walled garden with its bright flowers. It was warm there even in March. Did Valerie want to leave all that? He looked at Dad. Something was different. Dad's clothes were new and he was wearing jeans. His father was wearing *jeans*! And he was smiling. His father was Stephen Barber again. He was the bright and happy man who married Mum.

At dinner Dad tried hard to please Valerie. In the old days Dad didn't have to try to please women. They all loved him. The two girls who worked with him at the optician's loved him too.

Greg asked his mother about this once, but she wasn't unhappy about it. She just laughed. 'Oh, yes, they both love him,' she said.

'What about you?' Greg asked angrily.

'Oh, they think I don't understand him. I'm sure they'll be happy if I fall under a bus.'

But it wasn't a bus. She was driving her car when the accident happened. How did the two women in the optician's feel now? They were both young and beautiful. Valerie wasn't young or beautiful, but she was right, just right.

When he went up to bed that night, Greg left his door open and he could hear Dad and Valerie downstairs. They were talking and laughing together for hours.

It was very late when they came to bed.

⌀

So Dad was alive again. The next week he bought more clothes for himself and for Greg. His new clothes were much more fashionable than his old ones. And at the weekend he and

Valerie went out on Saturday and Sunday. Greg watched from his bedroom window. When they were getting into the car, Dad ran to open the door for Valerie. He no longer looked like a tired old man, Greg thought. In his new clothes, he looked slim and young.

On Wednesday Dad came home early and said he was going to a party. 'It's Yvonne at the shop,' he said. 'She's going to get married.'

'A party?' Greg said. 'You won't like the music, or the dancing. Yvonne's much younger than you, and you don't like my music. Is Valerie going?'

'Valerie? Of course not. I'm sure she's got better things to do.'

Greg thought back to the old days. Dad and Mum often went to quiet dinner parties with friends, but never to a party with dancing, with people who were twenty years younger. Greg didn't like it.

It was after midnight when Dad came home.

∞

Valerie came as usual on Friday. Greg cooked the dinner and then he went into the kitchen to get some drinks ready for them. But when Valerie arrived, Dad didn't hurry down to open the door as usual and Greg had to go himself. He took Valerie's bags from her and they went into the front room. Just then Greg heard Dad put the phone down in the bedroom upstairs.

After a while Dad came downstairs and went into the front room. Greg gave him some time alone with Valerie before he took the drinks in. But when he went in, they were just sitting and talking.

'I was just saying that I won't be here tomorrow,' Dad said. 'Well, not until the evening. I have to go to the shop. Sue phoned to say she can't come in to work.'

But later Greg remembered the sound of the phone upstairs. 'Nobody rang earlier,' he thought. 'Dad was making a call, not answering one.'

On Saturday morning Valerie said, 'You're cooking us a nice dinner tonight, Greg, so I'll make lunch today.'

Greg watched her for a minute while she sat at the kitchen table, cutting up apples. It was a comfortable, friendly picture, he thought. Then he ran upstairs to his father's bedroom, closed the door and phoned the optician's.

'Can I speak to Mr Barber, please?' he asked.

'I'm afraid he's not in today,' the girl answered. 'Can I help you?'

'No, it's nothing important, thank you,' Greg said.

But it *was* important. It was.

∝

On Sunday evening Valerie said, 'See you next week.' She was talking to Greg, but it was Dad who answered.

'I'm not sure. Can I phone you?'

'Yes, of course.' Valerie was a little surprised. Greg was very surprised – and at the same time, not surprised at all.

'What's happening next week, then?' he said after Valerie left. 'Where will we be?'

'Here . . . I don't know.' Dad wasn't looking at him. 'Well, perhaps I won't be here next weekend.'

'But I want to see Valerie next weekend.'

'Why don't you go there, then? I'll ask her, if you like.

Perhaps she's bored with coming here every week.'

'No, she isn't.'

'Look,' Dad said, 'Valerie's done a lot for us, she's a good friend, but, well, she's only a friend.'

'*Only* a friend? But I thought you – and her . . .'

'No.'

Later Greg told his friend, Toby, about it.

'Well, your Dad's free now,' Toby said. 'He's come alive again after your Mum's death, and he wants to start again. And Valerie's too old for him.'

'They're the same age. I asked her.'

'Yes, but she looks older than him. I've seen her. He doesn't want people to see him with someone like that. He can get someone better.'

The someone that Dad got was twenty-four and she looked eighteen.

'Oh, you are clever,' she said to Greg when he cooked the dinner that Friday evening. 'I can't cook anything.'

'Why don't you learn?' Greg said coldly. 'I won't always be here.' And neither will you, he said silently to himself.

WORD FOCUS

Complete the crossword with words from the story.

ACROSS

2 Greg said _____ _____ _____ music was in the 1950s. *(three words)*

7 Greg was surprised to see his father wearing _____.

9 Valerie brought a _____ _____ to Greg's house at Christmas. *(two words)*

10 Greg's father bought some new _____ clothes.

DOWN

1 Greg joined a _____ because he wanted to get out of the house sometimes.

3 Greg brought the _____ for the tree downstairs on Christmas Eve.

4 Greg's father is an _____, so he helps people with their glasses.

5 Greg's mother died in a car _____.

6 Greg went to band _____ at a friend's house.

8 The new clothes made Greg's father look _____ and young.

Story Focus

Here are three short passages from the story.
Read them and answer the questions.

'And what about that piece from the newspaper about older men losing their hair? You put that up on the kitchen wall! You've got to stop it.'

1 Who said these words in the story, and to whom?
2 Who put the piece from the newspaper on the wall?
3 Why do you think this person put it on the wall?

He wanted to give them more time together. He felt very pleased that his plan was going well.

4 In these sentences, who has a plan?
5 What is this plan?
6 Is this plan successful? If not, why do you think it isn't?

'Yes, but she looks older than him. I've seen her. He doesn't want people to see him with someone like that. He can get someone better.'

7 Who says these words in the story, and to whom?
8 Who are they talking about?
9 What do you think the speaker means by 'he can get someone better'?

31

A Walk
in Amnesia

~

If you have amnesia, you cannot remember who
you are. You don't know your own name, or where
you live, or if you have a sister or a brother, a wife
or a husband.

Elwyn Belford is a successful lawyer. He is
happily married, and has a good life. Perhaps he
works a little too hard sometimes. His doctor tells
him to be careful – working too hard can make
people very tired. They get ill, they forget who they
are. But Elwyn Belford is not worried. He feels very
well, very well indeed . . .

A Walk in Amnesia

Retold by Diane Mowat

That morning my wife and I said our usual goodbyes. She left her second cup of tea, and she followed me to the front door. She did this every day. She took from my coat a hair which was not there, and she told me to be careful. She always did this. I closed the door, and she went back to her tea.

I am a lawyer and I work very hard. My friend, Doctor Volney, told me not to work so hard. 'You'll be ill,' he said. 'A lot of people who work too hard get very tired, and suddenly they forget who they are. They can't remember anything. It's called amnesia. You need a change and a rest.'

'But I *do* rest,' I replied. 'On Thursday nights my wife and I play a game of cards, and on Sundays she reads me her weekly letter from her mother.'

That morning, when I was walking to work, I thought about Doctor Volney's words. I was feeling very well, and pleased with life.

❧

When I woke up, I was on a train and feeling very uncomfortable after a long sleep. I sat back in my seat and I tried to think. After a long time, I said to myself, 'I must have a name!' I looked in my pockets. No letter. No papers. Nothing with my name on. But I found three thousand dollars. 'I must be someone,' I thought.

34

The train was crowded with men who were all very friendly. One of them came and sat next to me. 'Hi! My name's R.P. Bolder – Bolder and Son, from Missouri. You're going to the meeting in New York, of course? What's your name?'

I had to reply to him, so I said quickly, 'Edward Pinkhammer from Cornopolis, Kansas.'

He was reading a newspaper, but every few minutes he looked up from it, to talk to me. I understood from his conversation that he was a druggist, and he thought that I was a druggist, too.

'Are all these men druggists?' I asked.

'Yes, they are,' he answered. 'Like us, they're all going to the yearly meeting in New York.'

After a time, he held out his newspaper to me. 'Look at that,' he said. 'Here's another of those men who run away and then say that they have forgotten who they are. A man gets tired of his business and his family, and he wants to have a good time. He goes away somewhere and when they find him, he says that he doesn't know who he is, and that he can't remember anything.'

I took the paper and read this:

Denver, June 12th
Elwyn C. Bellford, an important lawyer in the town, left home three days ago and has not come back. Just before he left, he took out a lot of money from his bank. Nobody has seen him since that day. He is a quiet man who enjoys his work and is happily married. But Mr Bellford works very hard, and it is possible that he has amnesia.

'But sometimes people do forget who they are, Mr Bolder,' I said.

'Oh, come on!' Mr Bolder answered. 'It's not true, you know! These men just want something more exciting in their lives – another woman, perhaps. Something different.'

We arrived in New York at about ten o'clock at night. I took a taxi to a hotel, and I wrote the name, 'Edward Pinkhammer', in the hotel book. Suddenly I felt wild and happy – I was free. A man without a name can do anything.

The young man behind the desk at the hotel looked at me a little strangely. I had no suitcase.

'I'm here for the Druggists' Meeting,' I said. 'My suitcase is lost.' I took out some money and gave it to him.

The next day I bought a suitcase and some clothes and I began to live the life of Edward Pinkhammer. I didn't try to remember who or what I was.

The next few days in Manhattan were wonderful – the theatres, the gardens, the music, the restaurants, the night life, the beautiful girls. And during this time I learned something very important – if you want to be happy, you must be free.

Sometimes I went to quiet, expensive restaurants with soft music. Sometimes I went on the river in boats full of noisy young men and their girlfriends. And then there was Broadway, with its theatres and bright lights.

One afternoon I was going back into my hotel when a fat man came and stood in front of me.

'Hello, Bellford!' he cried loudly. 'What are you doing in New York? Is Mrs B. with you?'

'I'm sorry, but you're making a mistake, sir,' I said coldly.

'My name is Pinkhammer. Please excuse me.' The man moved away, in surprise, and I walked over to the desk. Behind me, the man said something about a telephone.

'Give me my bill,' I said to the man behind the desk, 'and bring down my suitcase in half an hour.'

That afternoon I moved to a quiet little hotel on Fifth Avenue.

One afternoon, in one of my favourite restaurants on Broadway, I was going to my table when somebody pulled my arm.

'Mr Bellford,' a sweet voice cried.

I turned quickly and saw a woman who was sitting alone. She was about thirty and she had very beautiful eyes.

'How can you walk past me like that?' she said. 'Didn't you know me?'

I sat down at her table. Her hair was a beautiful red-gold colour.

'Are you sure you know me?' I asked.

'No.' She smiled. 'I never really knew you.'

'Well, my name is Edward Pinkhammer,' I said, 'and I'm from Kansas.'

'So, you haven't brought Mrs Bellford with you, then,' she said, and she laughed. 'You haven't changed much in fifteen years, Elwyn.'

Her wonderful eyes looked carefully at my face.

'No,' she said quietly, 'you haven't forgotten. I told you that you could never forget.'

'I'm sorry,' I answered, 'but that's the trouble. I *have* forgotten. I've forgotten everything.'

She laughed. 'Did you know that I married six months after you did? It was in all the newspapers.' She was silent for a minute. Then she looked up at me again. 'Tell me one thing, Elwyn,' she said softly. 'Since that night fifteen years ago, can you touch, smell, or look at white roses – and not think of me?'

'I can only say that I don't remember any of this,' I said carefully. 'I'm very sorry.' I tried to look away from her.

She smiled and stood up to leave. Then she held out her hand to me, and I took it for a second. 'Oh yes, you remember,' she said, with a sweet, unhappy smile.

'Goodbye, Elwyn Bellford.'

That night I went to the theatre and when I returned to my hotel, a quiet man in dark clothes was waiting for me.

'Mr Pinkhammer,' he said, 'can I speak with you for a minute? There's a room here.'

I followed him into a small room. A man and a woman were there. The woman was still beautiful, but her face was unhappy and tired. I liked everything about her. The man, who was about forty, came to meet me.

'Bellford,' he said, 'I'm happy to see you again. I told you that you were working too hard. Now you can come home with us. You'll soon be all right.'

'My name', I said, 'is Edward Pinkhammer. I've never seen you before in my life.'

The woman cried out, 'Oh, Elwyn! Elwyn! I'm your wife!' She put her arms round me, but I pushed them away.

'Oh, Doctor Volney! What is the matter with him?' the woman cried.

'Go to your room,' the doctor said to her. 'He'll soon be well again.'

The woman left, and so did the man in the dark clothes. The man who was a doctor turned to me and said quietly, 'Listen. Your name is not Edward Pinkhammer.'

'I know that,' I replied, 'but a man must have a name. Why not Pinkhammer?'

'Your name', the doctor said, 'is Elwyn Bellford. You are one of the best lawyers in Denver – and that woman is your wife.'

'She's a very fine woman,' I said, after a minute. 'I love the colour of her hair.'

'She's a very good wife,' the doctor replied. 'When you left two weeks ago, she was very unhappy. Then we had a telephone call from a man who saw you in a hotel here.'

'I think I remember him,' I said. 'He called me "Bellford". Excuse me, but who are you?'

'I'm Bobby Volney. I've been your friend for twenty years, and your doctor for fifteen years. Elwyn, try to remember.'

'You say you're a doctor,' I said. 'How can I get better? Does amnesia go slowly or suddenly?'

'Sometimes slowly. Sometimes suddenly.'

'Will you help me, Doctor Volney?' I asked.

'Old friend,' he said, 'I'll do everything possible.'

'Very well. And if you're my doctor, you can't tell anybody what I say.'

'Of course not,' Doctor Volney answered.

I stood up. There were some white roses on the table. I went over to the table, picked up the roses and threw them far out of the window. Then I sat down again.

'I think it will be best, Bobby,' I said, 'to get better suddenly. I'm a little tired of it all now. Go and bring my wife Marian in now. But, oh, Doctor,' I said with a happy smile. 'Oh, my good old friend – it was wonderful!'

WORD FOCUS

Use the clues below to help you complete this crossword with words from the story.

		1					2			
3		4			5					
					6			7		
8							9			
			10							

ACROSS

4 Elwyn meets a beautiful woman in a _____.

6 Elwyn leaves his home and goes to _____ _____ city. *(two words)*

8 Elwyn tells the man in the hotel that his _____ is lost.

9 The Doctor says to Elwyn, 'You need a change and a _____.'

10 Elwyn wakes up on a _____.

DOWN

1 On the train Elwyn meets a _____ from Missouri.

2 Elywn is a _____, and he works very hard.

3 Elwyn plays _____ on Thursday nights.

5 Elwyn forgets everything about his life because he has _____.

7 The beautiful woman talks to Elwyn about white _____.

Story Focus

Read the three endings for each of these sentences. All the endings are possible, but which one goes best with your understanding of the story? Choose one of them, and explain why you chose it.

1 Elwyn chose a new name for himself . . .
  a) because he could not remember his real name.
  b) because he wanted to be someone different for a while.
  c) because at first he wanted to start a new, more exciting life and never go back to his old life.

2 Elwyn said 'I've forgotten everything' to the woman with the red-gold hair . . .
  a) because he didn't want her to know that he was happy to see her again.
  b) because he didn't want to hurt the woman's feelings.
  c) because he did not remember her.

3 Elwyn threw the white roses out of the window . . .
  a) because he didn't care about the woman with the red-gold hair.
  b) because he remembered that night fifteen years ago, and it was very painful for him.
  c) because he still loved the woman with the red-gold hair and the roses made him want to be with her.

4 Elwyn wanted to 'get better suddenly' . . .
  a) because he was sorry to see his wife so unhappy.
  b) because after a good time and a nice rest he wanted to go back to his old life.
  c) because he knew his good friend Doctor Volney would keep his secret.

The
Five Orange Pips

~

Inside an orange there are pips, small white seeds hidden in the heart of the fruit. There is nothing very strange or mysterious about the pips of an orange. But it is strange to receive an envelope with five orange pips in it. And it is very worrying if, some years ago, your uncle and your father also received envelopes with five orange pips inside.

John Openshaw does not understand why somebody has sent him five orange pips, but he is afraid, very afraid. He knows he needs help, and so he goes to the great detective, Sherlock Holmes . . .

The Five Orange Pips

Retold by Clare West

1
The Story of Uncle Elias

In September 1887 my wife was visiting some of her family, so I was staying with my old friend Sherlock Holmes in Baker Street. It was a windy, stormy evening, and the rain was falling heavily outside. Suddenly there was a knock at the door.

I looked at my friend in surprise. 'Who can this be?' I asked.

'If he comes on business in this weather, it's important,' said Sherlock Holmes. 'Come in!' he called.

A young man came in. He looked wet, tired and worried. 'I've come to ask for help,' he said. 'I've heard of you, Mr Holmes. People say you know everything. I don't know what to do.'

'Well, sit down,' said Holmes, 'and tell me about yourself.'

The young man sat down, and put his wet feet near the fire. 'My name is John Openshaw. My father, Joseph, had a brother, my uncle Elias, who went to live in America when he was young. He made a lot of money there. He didn't like the black Americans, so during the Civil War he fought *against* the men from the North, and *with* those from the South. But when the South lost the war, and there was equality for black people, Uncle Elias left America. So in 1869 he came back to England and went to live in a large house in the country. He was a strange, unhappy man.

'He did not want any friends,' John Openshaw went on, 'and he often drank a lot. But he liked me, and when I was twelve, I moved to Uncle Elias's house. He was very kind to me. I could go anywhere in the house. But there was one small room at the top of the house which was always locked. Nobody could go into this room.

'One day Uncle Elias got a letter from Pondicherry in India. "I don't know anyone in Pondicherry!" he said, but when he opened the envelope, five little orange pips fell on to his plate. I began to laugh but stopped when I saw my uncle's white face.

' "K.K.K.!" he cried. "Oh my God, my God, they've found me!"

' "What do you mean, uncle?" I asked.

' "Death!" he cried, and ran upstairs.

'I looked at the envelope, which had three Ks on the back. There was no letter. Who sent it? And why was my uncle so afraid?

'Uncle Elias went immediately to the secret room and took out a box which also had three Ks on it. He burnt all the papers in the box, and said to me,

'"John, I know that I'm going to die soon. My brother, your father, will have all my money and my house after my death, and *you* will have it all when *he* dies. I hope you can enjoy it, but if not, give it to your worst enemy. I'm afraid that my money brings death with it."

'I didn't understand what he meant, and nothing happened for a few weeks, so I did not feel so worried. But my uncle was very afraid. He stayed in his room most of the time, and drank more than before. He always locked all the doors carefully. Then one night he drank very heavily and ran wildly out of the house, and in the morning we found him dead in a river. The police said he killed himself, but I knew he was afraid to die, so I didn't think that was true.'

Holmes stopped the young man for a minute. 'Tell me,' he said. 'When did your uncle get the letter from India, and when did he die?'

'The letter arrived on 10th March 1883, and he died seven weeks later,' answered John Openshaw.

'Thank you. Please go on,' said Holmes.

'After my uncle's death, my father moved into the house. Of course I asked him to look carefully at the locked room, but we didn't find anything important.'

2
More Pips

'Everything went well until a year later,' said John Openshaw. 'But one morning my father opened a letter to find five orange pips inside it. "What does this mean, John?" he asked. His face was white.

' "Look!" I said. "There's K.K.K. on the envelope. Those

letters were on Uncle Elias's envelope too!" We were both shaking and afraid.

' "Yes, and this time it says 'Put the papers in the garden'."

' "Which papers? The papers in Uncle Elias's box? He burnt them!" I said.

' "And where has this letter come from?" my father said. He looked at the envelope. "Dundee, Scotland. Well, I don't know anything about pips or papers. I'm not going to do anything."

' "Father, you must tell the police," I said.

'I remembered my uncle's letter from India, and I was very worried.

' "No, they'll laugh at me. Let's just forget about it," he replied.

'Three days later my poor father went to visit an old friend who lived some miles away. But he never came back. The police said that he was walking home in the dark when he fell down a hill. He was badly hurt, and he died soon after. They decided it was an accident, but I didn't agree. I thought it was murder, and I could not forget the five orange pips and the strange letters to my uncle and my father.

'But I've tried to forget, and I've lived alone in that house for nearly three years now. Then yesterday I got this.'

The young man showed us an envelope with K.K.K. on the back, and five small orange pips.

'You see?' he said. 'It comes from East London, and it says "Put the papers in the garden". Those are the words that were in the letter to my father.'

'So what did you do next?' asked Holmes.

'Nothing,' answered Openshaw. He put his head in his hands. 'I don't know what to do. I'm afraid.'

'Nothing?' cried Holmes. 'Young man, you must do something fast. You're in danger!'

'Well, I've talked to the police,' said Openshaw unhappily. 'But they laughed at me. They think that there's nothing to worry about.'

'How stupid they are!' cried Holmes. 'And why didn't you come to me immediately? Your enemies have had almost two days to make a plan. Haven't you found anything which will help us?'

'Well, I found this in the locked room,' said John Openshaw. He showed us a small, half-burnt piece of paper. 'It was with my uncle's papers. It's his writing. Look, it says:

March 7th 1869 Sent the pips to three people,
    Brown, Robinson and Williams.
March 9th Brown left.
March 10th Williams left.
March 12th Visited Robinson and finished business with him.

'Thank you,' said Sherlock Holmes. 'And now you must hurry home. Put this paper into your uncle's box, put in a letter which says that your uncle burnt all the other papers, and put the box outside in the garden. I hope your enemies will be happy with that, and then you won't be in danger any more. How are you going home?'

'By train from Waterloo station,' replied Openshaw.

'There'll be a lot of people in the streets, so I think that you'll be all right. But be careful.'

'Thank you, Mr Holmes,' said Openshaw. 'I'll do everything you say.' He went out into the dark night, the wind and the rain.

3
K.K.K.

Sherlock Holmes sat silently, and watched the fire. Then he said to me, 'John Openshaw is in real danger. Why did his Uncle Elias have to leave America? Because he had enemies. When he came back to England he was afraid. That's why he lived a lonely life and locked all his doors so carefully. Now where did those letters come from? Did you see?'

'The first from Pondicherry in India, the second from Dundee in Scotland and the third from East London,' I answered.

'Does that tell you anything?' asked Holmes.

'They're all sea ports. The writer was on a ship when he wrote the letters,' I replied. I was pleased with my answer.

'Very good, Watson,' said Holmes. 'Somebody sent some pips from India, and arrived seven weeks later to kill Uncle Elias. Then he sent some pips from Scotland and arrived three days later to kill John's father. Do you see why I'm worried now? He has sent pips to John *from London!* John's enemy is in London already!'

'Good God, Holmes!' I cried. 'Who is this man?'

'More than one man, I think. They belong to the Ku Klux Klan. That explains the "K.K.K.". Haven't you ever heard of it? It's a very secret group of Americans from the South. They wanted to stop equality for black people and to kill anyone who didn't agree with them. The police couldn't stop them. But in 1869 Uncle Elias, who belonged to this secret group, suddenly left America with all their papers, and so the group could not go on. Of course the group wanted to get the papers back. You remember the half-burnt paper? That was Uncle Elias's American diary. While he was working for the K.K.K., he sent the pips to frighten those three men. Two left the country, but one didn't, so the K.K.K. "finished business with him", or killed him. The K.K.K. always worked like that.'

'Well, I hope they won't kill young Openshaw,' I said.

4
The Last Deaths

But they did. The next morning we read in the newspaper that John Openshaw was dead. A policeman found him in the river near Waterloo station. The police said it was an accident, but Holmes was very angry about it.

'He came to me for help and those men murdered him! I'm going to find them, if it's the last thing I do!' he said to me, and he hurried out of the house.

In the evening, when he came back to Baker Street, he was tired, but pleased. 'Watson!' he said, 'I know the names of Openshaw's enemies! And now I'm going to send them a surprise! This will frighten them!' He took five pips from an orange and put them in an envelope. On it he wrote 'S.H. for J.C.'

'I'm sending the pips, not from the K.K.K., but from me, Sherlock Holmes, to Captain James Calhoun. His ship is called the *Star*. He and his men are sailing back to Georgia, USA, now.'

'How did you find him, Holmes?' I asked.

'Ship's papers,' he said. 'I've looked at hundreds of them today. Only one ship, the *Star*, was in the three ports at the right times, and this morning the *Star* left London to sail back to Georgia. I found out that the captain and two of his men, all Americans, weren't on the ship last night, so I'm sure they killed poor John Openshaw. When they arrive in America, they'll get the pips and then the police will catch them!'

Sherlock Holmes is a very clever detective, but he can do nothing about the weather. The winter storms at sea that year were worse than ever, and so the *Star* never arrived in Georgia, and nobody saw the captain or his men again. The murderers of John Openshaw did not get the pips, but, in the end, death came to them.

WORD FOCUS 1

Match each word with an appropriate meaning.

a small white seed found in fruit like oranges

civil war

to make someone afraid

envelope

a city or town by the sea where ships arrive and leave

equality

fighting between the people in one country

frighten

you put a letter inside this

pip

when black people and white people can

port

live together with no difficulty

WORD FOCUS 2

Perhaps Sherlock Holmes made some notes in his notebook while he was working on this case. Complete his notes with the words below.

case, Civil War, diary, envelope, equality, fought, frighten, killed, pips, ports, ship

The John Openshaw _____ began at the time of the American _____, when the North _____ against the South. John's uncle was a member of the K.K.K., a group of people who did not want _____ for blacks in America after the war. In his _____, John's uncle wrote that he sent orange _____ to three enemies of the K.K.K. He sent them

because he wanted to _____ the three men. Two of the men left the country, but the third did not, so he was _____. John's uncle, his father, and John each got an _____ with K.K.K. on the back and five pips inside. The pips came from different cities, but the cities were _____, so perhaps we must look for someone on a _____.

STORY FOCUS

> **SYMBOLS**
>
> The symbol for a dollar is **$**. The symbol ☑ is used to show that
> something is correct, and the symbol **=** means 'equal to'. Words can
> also be symbols. The word *red* means a colour, but the colour *red*
> can also make us think about other things like *love, anger, blood* . . .
> A word used like this is a SYMBOL.

The words and letters below can be symbols in English. Match them with
their related ideas. Are they also used as symbols in your language? Do they
have the same related ideas? Talk about your answers with a partner.

SYMBOLS   RELATED IDEAS

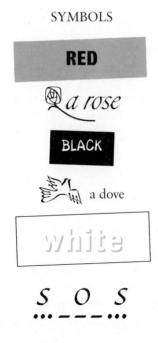

peace

pure

help!

love

ANGER

death

The
Tell-Tale Heart

~

I am mad, you are mad, we are all mad. I say you
are mad, you say I am mad. Everybody is mad.
Nobody is mad. How can we know what is true?
What does it *mean* to be mad?

Listen carefully to the voice in this story. Listen
to what he says, and if your blood runs cold, lock
your door at night, keep the light on, and do not let
your heart beat too loudly . . .

The Tell-Tale Heart

Retold by Margaret Naudi

It is true that I had been – and I am – very nervous, but do you really think that I am mad? I could see and hear *more* clearly – not less, because of the disease. My hearing, more than anything, was excellent. I could hear all things, things in this world and things in heaven. I heard many things in hell, too. So how can I be mad? See how clearly and calmly I can tell my story.

I cannot explain how the idea first came into my head. But once I had thought of the idea, I could not forget it. I had no reason to do it. I was not angry. I loved the old man. He had never hurt me in any way. I didn't want his gold. I think it was his eye! Yes! He had a pale blue eye, the eye of a vulture. Whenever I looked at it, my blood became cold; and so, very slowly, I decided to kill the old man and escape from the eye for ever.

You are thinking, I know, that I am mad. But madmen are not clever. And see how cleverly I prepared my plan! Every day that week I was so kind to the old man! And every night of that week, at about midnight, I opened his door very, very quietly. First I put my dark lantern through the opening of the door. The lantern was closed, and so no light came out of it, none at all. Then slowly, very slowly, I put my head inside the opening. I took sixty long minutes just to put my head inside. Would a madman have worked so carefully? And when my head was inside the room, I opened the lantern carefully and a thin ray of light fell onto the vulture eye. But the eye was always closed, so I could not do the work. You see, I did not hate the man; it was only the eye that I hated.

On the eighth night I started opening the door even more carefully. I was feeling calm and strong. There I was, opening his door, and he did not even know that I was there! I almost laughed at the idea. And perhaps, at that moment, he heard me, because he suddenly moved in his bed. But I did not move away. I knew that he could not see the opening of the door, so I continued pushing it open, slowly and quietly.

When my head was in the room, I tried to open the lantern but my thumb slipped and I made a noise. Immediately, the man sat up in bed and shouted, 'Who's there?'

I said nothing. For an hour I just stood there, without moving, and he sat in his bed, listening. Then he made a soft noise, a noise which I recognized. It was the noise of terror, the terror of death. I knew the sound because I had made it myself, many times, in the deep of the night, when all the world was asleep. I felt sorry for the old man, but I laughed silently. I knew that he had been awake since the first noise, and his fear had grown and grown. Death had entered his room, and now the shadow of death lay all around him. He could neither see me nor hear me, but he could *feel* my head inside his room.

I opened the lantern a little and a thin ray of light fell on his eye. It was open, and as I looked at it, I became angry. I could see it clearly, a horrible, pale blue eye that turned my blood cold. I could see nothing of the man's face or body, just his eye.

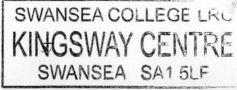

And then I heard a sound. Hadn't I told you that my hearing was excellent? I knew the sound. It was the beating of the old man's heart. It grew louder and quicker. Yes, louder and louder with every minute. The old man's terror must have been very great. And now a new terror came to me – a neighbour might hear the noise of this beating heart! The old man's time had come!

I opened the lantern fully and ran into the room. He shouted once – but only once because I pulled him to the floor and pulled the heavy bed over him. For many minutes the heart continued to beat, but then it stopped. The old man was dead. I put my hand on his heart and held it there for many minutes. There was no life in him at all. Now his eye would not trouble me again.

Perhaps you are still thinking that I am mad. You will not, when I tell you of the clever way I hid the body. First, I cut it into pieces. I cut off the head and the arms and the legs. I then took up three boards from the wooden floor, and hid the body underneath. Finally, I replaced the wooden boards with great care. Now no human eye – not even *his* – would see anything wrong. There was nothing to see – not even any blood. A bowl had caught it all – ha! ha!

When I finished, it was four o'clock and it was still dark. There was a knock at the front door. Calmly, because I knew I had nothing to fear, I opened the door. Three policemen came in. They had come because a neighbour had reported a loud shout coming from the house.

I welcomed the policemen and asked them to come in. I explained that it was I who had shouted, in a dream. The old man, I said, was away in the country. I took them round the house and asked them to search it well. Then I took them to the old man's room and showed them all his things. I brought chairs into the room and invited them to sit down and rest a while. Calmly, I put my own chair on the place where I had hidden his body.

The policemen seemed happy. They could see from the way I spoke that all was well. They continued talking, but I began to get tired. My head ached, and there was a ringing noise in my ears. I wanted the men to go away, but they continued to talk. The ringing became louder and clearer. And then I realized that the noise was *not* in my ears.

I became very pale, and starting talking more loudly. But the noise became louder too. What could I do? It was a low, soft sound, like the sound made by a watch when it is covered in cotton. I spoke more loudly. The noise became louder too. Why, oh why, didn't the men go away? I walked up and down the room. I became angry, I argued, I threw the chair onto the floor. But the noise continued to grow louder, louder than every noise I made. And the men went on talking and smiling. Was it possible that they hadn't heard the terrible noise? No! no! They heard! *They knew!* They were only pretending that they hadn't heard the noise! I was sure of this – I still am – and I hated their smiling faces. I felt that I must scream or die! And now, again, the noise was louder, louder, *louder*!

'Stop!' I shouted. 'Stop pretending that you cannot hear it! Yes, I did it! Pull up the floorboards here! here, here! – it is the beating of his horrible heart!'

WORD FOCUS

Match each word with an appropriate meaning. Then use nine of the eleven words to complete the passage below. (Use one word in each gap.)

light in colour

boards

with a sick mind

heaven

a thin line of light

hell

very great fear

lantern

to move suddenly by accident and fall or almost fall

mad

nervous

the home of God, where many people believe they will go when they die

pale

ray

long thin flat pieces of wood

slip

a large bird that eats dead animals

terror

a light in a closed glass box

vulture

the place where bad people go when they die

afraid, worried

When I was in the old man's house, I was always very _____. And I could hear very clearly. In fact, I could hear many things in _____ and _____, but I do not think that I was _____. I liked the old man. But I really hated his eye because it had a _____ blue colour, and it looked like a _____'s eye. Every night at midnight, I went to the old man's room and used a _____ to see the terrible eye. One night, the old man woke up, and I knew that he felt the _____ of death. Then I heard his beating heart, and ran into the room. When the old man was dead, I cut up his body, and put it under the floor _____. But I couldn't stop the noise . . .

STORY FOCUS 1

In a story, the narrator is a character who tells the story. What do you think about the narrator of *The Tell-Tale Heart*? Choose one of these adjectives for the first gap, and then write as much as you like to finish the sentences.

angry, calm, careful, clever, horrible, kind, mad, nervous, strong

1 I think the narrator was _____ because _____.
2 The narrator was _____ when _____.
3 The narrator says that he is _____, but I think _____.
4 The narrator wasn't _____ when _____.
5 After he kills the old man, the narrator is _____ because _____.

STORY FOCUS 2

Match these halves of sentences to make a paragraph of five sentences. Who do you think the narrator is here?

1 When we first arrived at the house, . . .
2 He seemed very calm and I believed his story at first, . . .
3 There's something very strange about this man . . .
4 Why has he thrown his chair onto the floor . . .
5 We'll just continue to sit here and talk and wait . . .

6 . . . and begun to talk so loudly and angrily?
7 . . . but now I am not so sure.
8 . . . because I think we will learn something very soon.
9 . . . the man explained that he had shouted out in a dream.
10 . . . and I'm beginning to think that he's mad.

Go, Lovely Rose

~

If you are a parent, you worry about your children. You worry even when they are nearly adult. Are they safe? Are they happy? Where are they? Why haven't they come home? It is long past midnight, and who *is* this man who has taken my daughter out to a dance?

In a rose garden on a warm summer night, a father waits for his daughter to come home. He watches, and waits, and worries . . .

Go, Lovely Rose

Retold by Rosemary Border

'**B**ut who is she with?' said Mr Carteret.

'A young man. She met him on the aeroplane,' Mrs Carteret said. 'Now go to sleep.'

Outside the bedroom window the moon was shining brightly.

'Nobody told me there was a young man on the aeroplane,' said Mr Carteret crossly.

'You saw him,' Mrs Carteret said. 'He was there when you met her at the airport.'

'I don't remember,' said her husband.

'Yes, you do. You noticed his hat. You said so. It was a light green . . .'

'Oh dear!' said Mr Carteret. 'That man? But he's too old for her. He must be nearly forty.'

'He's twenty-eight, dear. Now go to sleep.'

'I can't sleep,' said Mr Carteret. 'Three o'clock in the morning and I can't get to sleep.'

'Just lie still, dear, and you'll soon fall asleep,' said his wife.

It was a warm night in July. A gentle wind whispered in the trees outside the bedroom window. It sounded like a car coming. Mr Carteret sat up and listened. But it was only the wind.

'Where are you going now?' said Mrs Carteret.

'I'm going downstairs for a drink of water. I can't sleep. I can never sleep in moonlight – I don't know why. And it's very hot too.'

'Put your slippers on,' said Mrs Carteret sleepily.

He found his slippers and put them on. He went down to the kitchen and turned on the tap. The water was warmish. He let the water run until it was cool enough to drink. Then he opened the kitchen door and went out into the garden. The moon shone on his roses. Mr Carteret could see the shape and colour of every flower. There they were: red and yellow and white, very soft and sweet-smelling. Each flower was wet with dew.

He stood on the short green grass and looked up at the sky. The moon was very bright. It was like a strong, white electric light shining down on the garden.

The wind whispered again in the trees. Again Mr Carteret thought it was a car coming. Suddenly he felt helpless and miserable.

'Sue,' he said aloud, 'Sue . . . where are you? What are you doing? Susie, Susie, you don't usually stay out so late.'

Susie. He always called her Susie when he was specially pleased with her. Usually he called her Sue. When he was cross with her, he called her Susan.

He remembered her nineteenth birthday, three weeks before. She was getting ready to fly off to Switzerland for a holiday.

'How lovely she is!' everyone said. 'How pretty and grown-up! And she's going to Switzerland all by herself! How wonderful!'

But Mr Carteret did not think his daughter looked grown-up. To him she looked smaller and more girlish than ever. 'Too young to go away by herself,' he thought crossly.

He heard the church clock. Half past three. At that moment he heard the sound of a car. This time he was sure. He could see its lights coming along the road.

'You're late, young lady,' he said to himself. He did not feel miserable any more; just a little cross. He could hear the car coming quickly along the road. Suddenly he began to run towards the house. He did not want her to find him there. He wanted to get back to bed. His pyjama trousers were too long. They were wet with dew. He held them up, like skirts, as he ran.

'This is stupid,' he thought. 'What stupid things parents do sometimes!'

At the kitchen door one of his slippers fell off. He stopped to pick it up, and listened again for the sound of the car. All was quiet. Once again he was alone in the quiet, moonlit garden. His slippers were wet with dew. His wet pyjama trousers felt uncomfortable on his legs.

'It didn't stop,' he thought. He felt cross and miserable again. '*We* always walked home from dances,' he said aloud. 'That was part of the fun.'

Suddenly he felt frightened. He remembered the corner on the road near his house. 'It's a dangerous corner,' he said to himself. 'There are accidents there every week. What if Susie and this man . . .' He did not want to think about it. It was too awful.

'And who *is* this man anyway? How do I know he's a suitable friend for Susie? Perhaps he's a married man. Or a criminal.'

All at once he had a terrible feeling about this man. 'I felt like this when I saw her getting into the aeroplane,' he thought.

'I had a feeling of . . . of danger . . . accidents.' He was shaking now. He felt cold and sick. 'She's had a crash in that man's car,' he thought. 'I'm sure of it.'

Now he was walking backwards and forwards across the dewy, moonlit grass. 'I'm sure she's had an accident,' he thought. 'In a minute or two the police will telephone – oh dear! oh dear!'

He began to walk up the road in his pyjamas and bedroom slippers. He looked at the sky; there were lines of gold above the tree-tops. The moon was disappearing. It was almost day. 'Oh, where *is* she?' he cried, and he began to run.

A few moments later, he thought he saw a pair of yellow eyes looking at him from the road. He realized that they were the lights of a car. It was standing at the side of the road. He did not know what to do about it. Should he go up to the car, and knock on the window and say, 'Susan, come home'? But there was always the chance that some other man's daughter was in the car.

'And then what will she think of me – out here in my pyjamas?'

He stopped and watched the light of day filling the sky. 'What will the neighbours think if they see me?' he thought. 'I must go home and get to bed. I don't know why I'm worrying like this. I never worried like this when she was little.'

He turned and started to walk home. Just then he heard a car engine. He looked round and saw its lights coming along the road. Suddenly he felt more stupid than ever. There was no time to get away. He could only hide behind a tree. The long wet grass under the tree made his pyjamas wetter than ever.

The car passed him. He could not see who was inside. 'Perhaps it's Susie,' he thought. 'And now I shall have to go home and change my pyjamas.' He started walking again. Then he stopped once more. 'What if it isn't Susie?' he thought. 'What if something really has happened to Susie?'

He felt sick and cold and miserable. The blood seemed to whisper and sing inside his ears. His heart seemed to fill his whole body.

'Oh, Susie,' he whispered, 'Come home safely. Please . . .'

He realized that the car had stopped outside his house. A moment later he saw Susie. She was wearing her long yellow evening dress. 'How pretty she is!' he thought. He heard her sweet, girlish voice calling: 'Goodbye. Yes. Lovely. Thank you.'

'I mustn't let her see me now,' he thought. 'I must keep out of sight. I must go in through the back door. Then I can go upstairs and put on dry pyjamas . . .'

A moment later the car turned and came back along the road towards him. This time there was no chance to hide. For a few miserable moments he stood there with the lights of the car shining in his eyes.

'Look natural,' he said to himself. 'And hope that nobody notices me.'

The car stopped and a voice called out:

'Excuse me, sir. Are you Mr Carteret?'

'Yes,' he said. 'I'm Carteret.' He tried to sound cool and unworried.

'Oh. I'm Bill Jordan, sir. I'm sorry we were so late. I hope you haven't been worried about Susie?'

'Oh! No. Of course not.'

'My mother kept us, you see.'

'But I thought you went to a dance.'

'Oh no, sir. We went to dinner with my mother. We played cards until three o'clock. My mother loves cards. She forgot the time.'

'Oh, that's all right. I hope you had a good time.'

'Oh, we had a wonderful time, thank you. But I thought that perhaps you were worried about Susie . . .'

'No, no. Of course not!'

'That's all right then.' The young man looked at Mr Carteret's wet pyjamas and looked away again. 'It's been a wonderfully warm night, hasn't it?' he said politely.

'Terribly hot. I couldn't sleep.'

'Sleep! I must get home to bed!' He smiled, showing beautiful white teeth. 'Good night, sir.'

'Good night.'

The car began to move away. The young man waved goodbye and Mr Carteret called after him:

'You must come and have dinner with us one evening . . .'

'How kind! Yes, please . . . Good night, sir.'

Mr Carteret walked down the road. 'He called me sir,' he thought. 'What a polite young man! I like him.'

He reached the garden. The new light of morning shone on his roses. There was one very beautiful red rose, newly opened and dark as blood. 'I'll pick it,' he said to himself, 'and take it upstairs for my wife.' But, in the end, he decided to leave it there.

And then suddenly, a bird began to sing.

WORD FOCUS

Perhaps Susie talked to her mother the next day about her father and Bill. Complete their conversation with these words. (Use one word in each gap.)

grown, guy, helpless, holiday, polite, problems, pyjamas, suitable, trust, worries, wrong

SUSIE: Bill said that when he brought me home last night he saw dad outside in his _____. He wasn't waiting for me, was he?

MOTHER: Well Susie, you know that your father still _____ about you, and it was very late.

SUSIE: But I'm not a little girl any more! Can't he see that I've _____ up?

MOTHER: Well, he did let you go to Switzerland for a _____ by yourself. While you were away, he felt really _____ because he didn't know if you were in trouble, or if you needed help.

SUSIE: But I didn't have any _____, and I met a great _____ on the aeroplane.

MOTHER: That's true. At first your father thought that Bill wasn't _____ for you because he's too old. But after he met Bill outside, he changed his mind.

SUSIE: Do you mean he likes Bill?

MOTHER: When your father came in last night, he said, 'I met Bill outside, and he was very _____. He's a fine young man. I was _____ about him.'

SUSIE: I can't believe it! Maybe dad will finally start to _____ me.

STORY FOCUS

Here is Susie the next day, using her computer to chat with her friend Tina about her night out with Bill, and her problem with her father. Complete what Susie and Tina say, using as many words as you like.

Susie says:	17:43:28

Hi, Tina, I really need to talk to you. Are you online now?

Tina says:	17:44:15

Hi, Susie, I'm here. Is something wrong?

Susie says:	17:45:39

Oh, I'm so angry with my dad. Last night, after Bill brought me home, he was driving away from the house when he saw _____.

Tina says:	17:48:50

In his pyjamas?! Why, what time was it?

Susie says:	17:52:24

About half past three in the morning. But I was so embarrassed when

_____.

Tina says:	17:54:08

Half past three, Susie! Of course your father _____.

Susie says:	17:56:31

Yes, but I'm _____. And anyway, we were only _____.

Tina says:	17:59:02

Yes, but your father didn't know that, did he? You've got to remember that fathers _____.

Susie says:	18:01:23

Yes, I know, but I wish _____.

Tina says:	18:03:48

Ah, come on, Susie! Your father loves you. He's only thinking about you! Now, please tell me ALL about Bill! Every little detail!

About the
Authors

~

O. HENRY

O. Henry (1862–1910), whose real name was William Sydney Porter, was born in North Carolina in the USA. When he was twenty, he went to Texas and worked in many different offices and then in a bank. In 1887 he married a young woman called Athol Estes, and he and Athol were very happy together. His most famous short story is *The Gift of the Magi* (called *The Christmas Presents* in this book), and many people think that Della in this story is based on his wife Athol.

In 1896 Porter ran away to Honduras because people said he stole money from the bank when he was working there in 1894. A year later he came back to Texas to see his wife Athol, who was dying, and in 1898 he was sent to prison. During his time there he published many short stories, and when he left prison in 1901, he was already a famous writer.

Porter's stories are both sad and funny, and show a great understanding of the everyday lives of ordinary people. He wrote about six hundred stories and made a lot of money, but he was a very unhappy man. When he died, he had only twenty-three cents in his pocket, and his last words were:

'Turn up the lights; I don't want to go home in the dark.'

THOMAS HARDY

Thomas Hardy (1840–1928) was born in a small village in Dorset, in the south of England. When he was a young man, he often played the fiddle at weddings and parties, and he loved listening to old people telling stories of country life. Later, Hardy put many of the characters and events from these stories into his own short stories and novels.

At twenty-two, he went to London to work as an architect, and there he started writing poems, stories, and novels. His fourth novel, *Far from the Madding Crowd*, was very popular, and from this he earned enough money to stop working and also to get married. He wrote several other successful novels, but some readers did not like them, saying they were dark and cruel. After this, Hardy stopped writing novels and returned to poetry.

For most of his life, he lived in Dorset with his first wife, Emma. Soon after she died, he married again. After his death his heart was buried in Emma's grave.

JAN MARK

Jan Mark (1943–2006) was born in Hertfordshire, England. She studied art and design, and was an art teacher before she became a writer. Her first book, *Thunder and Lightnings*, won the Carnegie Medal (an important prize for the best children's book of the year). She wrote picture books, novels, plays, and television plays, and her books won several prizes. The story in this book, *Too Old to Rock and Roll*, comes from her short-story collection *A Can of Worms*.

Readers of all ages enjoy Jan Mark's stories. She herself said: 'I write about children, but I don't mind who reads the books.' Many of her stories are about friends – making friends, losing friends, learning to live with friends. People like her books because of her deep understanding of children and teenagers, and the funny, difficult, and painful things that happen in their lives.

SIR ARTHUR CONAN DOYLE

Sir Arthur Conan Doyle (1859–1930) was born in Edinburgh, Scotland. He studied medicine and worked as a doctor for eight years. He started writing because he wanted to earn more money, and soon people were reading his stories in weekly magazines. In Conan Doyle's first novel, *A Study in Scarlet*, Sherlock Holmes appeared for the first time – a strange, but very clever detective. He can find the answer to almost any problem, and likes to explain the mysteries to his slow-thinking friend, Dr. Watson. Conan Doyle preferred writing novels about history, and he soon became bored with the Sherlock Holmes character. So, in *The Final Problem*, he 'killed' him, and Holmes and his famous enemy, Moriarty, fell to their deaths on a mountain. But people wanted more stories about Holmes, and Conan Doyle had to bring him back to life, in *The Hound of the Baskervilles* in 1902.

There are more than fifty short stories about Sherlock Holmes, and many plays and films about the great detective.

EDGAR ALLAN POE

Edgar Allan Poe (1809–1849) was born in Boston, USA. His parents died when he was young, and he went to live with the Allan family in Richmond. He spent a year at university and then two years in the army. In 1831, he moved to Baltimore to live with his aunt and his cousin Virginia. For the next few years, life was difficult. He sold some stories to magazines, but they brought him little money. But he did find happiness with Virginia, whom he married in 1836.

From 1838 to 1844, Poe lived in Philadelphia, where he wrote some of his most famous horror stories. Then he moved to New York, where his poem, *The Raven*, soon made him famous. But Virginia died in 1847, and Poe began drinking heavily. He tried to kill himself in 1848 and died the following year.

Poe wrote many different kinds of stories, and his horror stories are only a small part of his work. But to most people the name Edgar Allan Poe means stories of death and madness, horror and ghosts.

H. E. BATES

Herbert Ernest Bates (1905–1974) was born in Northamptonshire, England. His family were shoe-makers. After leaving school, he worked as a newspaper reporter and then in a shoe factory warehouse. He was often alone in the office, and this is where he wrote his first novel, *The Two Sisters*.

During the Second World War, Bates joined the Royal Air Force, and he also worked as the Armed Forces' first short-story writer. He wrote under the name 'Flying Officer X'. His most famous novel, published in 1944, is about the crew of a British plane shot down in France. Bates also wrote about his war-time experiences in Burma.

For fifty years, Bates published at least one new novel or collection of short stories each year. He lived in the countryside of Kent, and like some of his characters, he is remembered as a passionate Englishman, with a deep love for the countryside and the beauty of nature.

READING CIRCLE ROLES

When you work on your role sheet, remember these words:

~ READ ~ THINK ~ CONNECT ~ ASK ~~ AND CONNECT

READ ~
- Read the story once without stopping.
- Read it again while you work on your role sheet.

THINK ~
- Look for passages in the story that are interesting or unusual. Think about them. Prepare some questions to ask about them.
- Think about the meanings of words. If you use a dictionary, try to use an English-to-English learner's dictionary.

CONNECT ~
- Connect with the characters' thoughts and feelings. Perhaps it is a horror story and we cannot 'connect' with an experience like this, but we can see how the characters are thinking or feeling.

ASK ~
- Ask questions with many possible answers; questions that begin with *How? Why? What? Who?* Do not ask *yes/no* questions.
- When you ask questions, use English words that everyone in your circle can understand, so that everyone can talk about the story.

AND CONNECT ~
- Connect with your circle. Share your ideas, listen to other people's ideas. If you don't understand something, ask people to repeat or explain. And have fun!

The role sheets are on the next six pages (and on page 90 there are role badges you can make). Bigger role sheets, with space for writing, are in the Teacher's Handbook. Or you can read about your role in these pages, and write your notes and questions in your own notebook.

Discussion Leader

STORY: _____

NAME: _____

The Discussion Leader's job is to . . .

• read the story twice, and prepare at least five general questions about it.
• ask one or two questions to start the Reading Circle discussion.
• make sure that everyone has a chance to speak and joins in the discussion.
• call on each member to present their prepared role information.
• guide the discussion and keep it going.

Usually the best discussion questions come from your own thoughts, feelings, and questions as you read. (What surprised you, made you smile, made you feel sad?) Write down your questions as soon as you have finished reading. It is best to use your own questions, but you can also use some of the ideas at the bottom of this page.

MY QUESTIONS:

1 _____

— _____

— _____

— _____

— _____

— _____

— _____

Other general ideas:

• Questions about the characters (*like / not like them, true to life / not true to life ...?*)
• Questions about the theme (*friendship, romance, parents/children, ghosts ...?*)
• Questions about the ending (*surprising, expected, liked it / did not like it ...?*)
• Questions about what will happen next. (These can also be used for a longer story.)

Summarizer

STORY: _____

NAME: _____

The Summarizer's job is to . . .

- read the story and make notes about the characters, events, and ideas.
- find the key points that everyone must know to understand and remember the story.
- retell the story in a short summary (one or two minutes) in your own words.
- talk about your summary to the group, using your writing to help you.

Your reading circle will find your summary very useful, because it will help to remind them of the plot and the characters in the story. You may need to read the story more than once to make a good summary, and you may need to repeat it to the group a second time.

MY KEY POINTS:

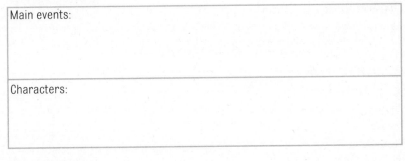

Main events:

Characters:

MY SUMMARY:

Connector

STORY: _____

NAME: _____

The Connector's job is to . . .

- read the story twice, and look for connections between the story and the world outside.
- make notes about at least two possible connections to your own experiences, or to the experiences of friends and family, or to real-life events.
- tell the group about the connections and ask for their comments or questions.
- ask the group if they can think of any connections themselves.

These questions will help you think about connections while you are reading.
Events: Has anything similar ever happened to you, or to someone you know? Does anything in the story remind you of events in the real world? For example, events you have read about in newspapers, or heard about on television news programmes.
Characters: Do any of them remind you of people you know? How? Why? Have you ever had the same thoughts or feelings as these characters have? Do you know anybody who thinks, feels, behaves like that?

MY CONNECTIONS:

1 _____

— _____

— _____

— _____

— _____

— _____

— _____

— _____

— _____

Word Master

STORY: _____

NAME: _____

The Word Master's job is to . . .

- read the story, and look for words or short phrases that are new or difficult to understand, or that are important in the story.
- choose five words (only five) that you think are important for this story.
- explain the meanings of these five words in simple English to the group.
- tell the group why these words are important for understanding this story.

Your five words do not have to be new or unknown words. Look for words in the story that really stand out in some way. These may be words that are:

- repeated often   • used in an unusual way   • important to the meaning of the story

MY WORDS	MEANING OF THE WORD	REASON FOR CHOOSING THE WORD
PAGE_____ LINE _____		
PAGE_____ LINE _____		
PAGE_____ LINE _____		
PAGE_____ LINE _____		
PAGE_____ LINE _____		

Passage Person

STORY: _____

NAME: _____

The Passage Person's job is to . . .

- read the story, and find important, interesting, or difficult passages.
- make notes about at least three passages that are important for the plot, or that explain the characters, or that have very interesting or powerful language.
- read each passage to the group, or ask another group member to read it.
- ask the group one or two questions about each passage.

A passage is usually one paragraph, but sometimes it can be just one or two sentences, or perhaps a piece of dialogue. You might choose a passage to discuss because it is:

• important   • informative   • surprising   • funny   • confusing   • well-written

MY PASSAGES:

PAGE _____ LINES _____

REASONS FOR CHOOSING THE PASSAGE	QUESTIONS ABOUT THE PASSAGE

PAGE _____ LINES _____

REASONS FOR CHOOSING THE PASSAGE	QUESTIONS ABOUT THE PASSAGE

PAGE _____ LINES _____

REASONS FOR CHOOSING THE PASSAGE	QUESTIONS ABOUT THE PASSAGE

Culture Collector

STORY: _____

NAME: _____

The Culture Collector's job is to . . .

• read the story, and look for both differences and similarities between your own culture and the culture found in the story.
• make notes about two or three passages that show these cultural points.
• read each passage to the group, or ask another group member to read it.
• ask the group some questions about these, and any other cultural points in the story.

Here are some questions to help you think about cultural differences.
Theme: What is the theme of this story (for example, getting married, meeting a ghost, murder, unhappy children)? Is this an important theme in your own culture? Do people think about this theme in the same way, or differently?
People: Do characters in this story say or do things that people never say or do in your culture? Do they say or do some things that everybody in the world says or does?

MY CULTURAL COLLECTION (differences and similarities)

1 **PAGE** _____ **LINES** _____ : _____

_____

2 **PAGE** _____ **LINES** _____ : _____

_____

MY CULTURAL QUESTIONS

1 _____

__ _____

__ _____

__ _____

PLOT PYRAMID ACTIVITY

A **plot** is a series of events which form a story. The Reading Circles **Plot Pyramid** is a way of looking at and talking about the plot of a story. The pyramid divides the story into five parts.

The Exposition gives the background needed to understand the story. It tells us who the characters are, where the story happens, and when it happens. Sometimes we also get an idea about problems to come.

The Complication is the single event which begins the conflict, or creates the problem. The event might be an action, a thought, or words spoken by one of the characters.

The Rising Action brings more events and difficulties. As the story moves through these events, it gets more exciting, and begins to take us toward the climax.

The Climax is the high point of the story, the turning point, the point of no return. It marks a change, for better or for worse, in the lives of one or more of the characters.

The Resolution usually offers an answer to the problem or the conflict, which may be sad or happy for the characters. Mysteries are explained, secrets told, and the reader can feel calm again.

HOW TO PLOT THE PYRAMID

1 Read your story again, and look for each part of the pyramid as you read. Make notes, or mark your book.

2 In your Reading Circle, find each part of the pyramid in the story, and then write down your ideas. Use the boxes in the diagram opposite as a guide (a bigger diagram, with space for writing in the boxes, is in the Teacher's Handbook).

3 Begin with the *Exposition*, and work through the *Complication*, the *Rising Action* (only two points), the *Climax*, and the *Resolution*.

4 Finally, your group draws the pyramid and writes the notes on the board, and then presents the pyramid to the class.

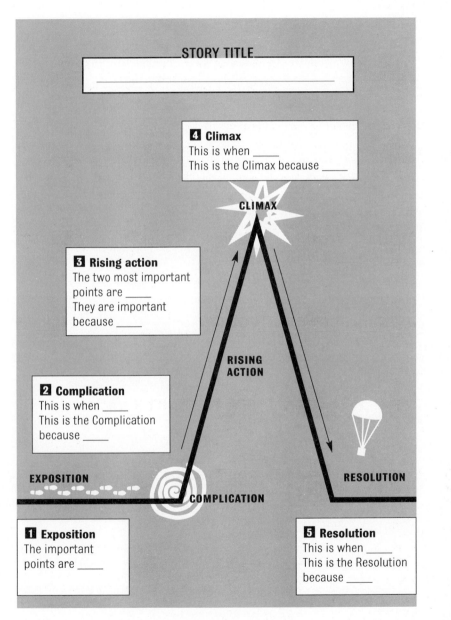

STORY TITLE

4 Climax
This is when _____
This is the Climax because _____

CLIMAX

3 Rising action
The two most important
points are _____
They are important
because _____

RISING
ACTION

2 Complication
This is when _____
This is the Complication
because _____

EXPOSITION

RESOLUTION

COMPLICATION

1 Exposition
The important
points are _____

5 Resolution
This is when _____
This is the Resolution
because _____

POSTER ACTIVITY

Each Reading Circle group makes a poster in English about a story in this book. Posters can have words, pictures, and drawings. Your group will need to find extra information about the story – perhaps from the Internet, or the school library, or your teacher.

Use the ideas on the opposite page to help you. When all the posters are finished, each Reading Circle will present their own poster to the other groups. At the end, keep all the posters, and make a 'poster library'.

STORY TITLE

THE THEME
What is the theme of the story?

- Is it about love or murder or friendship? Is it about dreams or wishes or fears?

THE TIME, THE PLACE
What do you know about the time and the place of the story?

- the city / the country?
- a real world, or an unreal world?
- If the time and place are not given, does it matter?

THE WRITER
What interesting facts do you know about the author's life?

- Was he or she also a poet, an actor, a teacher? Or a spy, a sailor, a thief, a doctor, a madman?

THE BACKGROUND
What cultural information did you learn from the story?

- About family events (for example, a wedding)
- A national holiday
- Family life (for example, parents and children)

THE LANGUAGE
What did you like about the language in the story?

- Find a quotation you like – words that are funny or clever or sad, or words that paint a picture in your mind.

THE FILM
Direct your own film! Who will play the characters in the film?

- Choose the best actors to play the characters.
- Where will you film it?
- Will you change the story?
- What title will the film have?

BOOKWORMS CLUB BRONZE
Stories for Reading Circles
STAGES 1 AND 2
Editor: Mark Furr

In these seven short stories there are marriages and murder, mistakes and mysteries. People fall in love, and fall out of love; they argue, and talk, and laugh, and cry. They go travelling, they go dancing – they even see ghosts. All of human life is here . . .

The Bookworms Club brings together a selection of adapted short stories from other Bookworms titles. These stories have been specially chosen for use with Reading Circles.

The Horse of Death
Sait Faik, from *Four Turkish Stories*

The Little Hunters at the Lake
Yalvac Ural, from *Four Turkish Stories*

Mr Harris and the Night Train
Jennifer Bassett, from *One-Way Ticket*

Sister Love
John Escott, from *Sister Love and Other Crime Stories*

Omega File 349: London, England
Jennifer Bassett, from *The Omega Files*

Tildy's Moment
O. Henry, from *New Yorkers*

Andrew, Jane, the Parson, and the Fox
Thomas Hardy, from *Tales from Longpuddle*

BOOKWORMS CLUB GOLD
Stories for Reading Circles
STAGES 3 AND 4
Editor: Mark Furr

In these seven short stories there are many different answers to life's little problems. How to plan the perfect murder – and succeed. How to choose – and keep – the perfect wife or husband. How to find hidden gold. How to live for two hundred years . . .

The Bookworms Club brings together a selection of adapted short stories from other Bookworms titles. These stories have been specially chosen for use with Reading Circles.

The Black Cat
Edgar Allan Poe, from *Tales of Mystery and Imagination*

Sredni Vashtar
Saki, from *Tooth and Claw*

The Railway Crossing
Freeman Wills Crofts, from *As the Inspector Said and Other Stories*

The Daffodil Sky
H. E. Bates, from *Go, Lovely Rose and Other Stories*

A Moment of Madness
Thomas Hardy, from *The Three Strangers and Other Stories*

The Secret
Arthur C. Clarke, from *The Songs of Distant Earth and Other Stories*

The Experiment
M. R. James, from *The Unquiet Grave*

ROLE BADGES

These role icons can be photocopied and then cut out to make badges or stickers for the members of the Reading Circle to wear.